THE URBAN MINISTRY INSTITUTE, a ministry of WORLD IMPACT, INC.

WAR OF THE WORLDS

SIAFU
MEN'S CONFERENCE
2012
REV. DR. DON L. DAVIS

TUMI Press
3701 East Thirteenth Street North
Wichita, Kansas 67208

Table of Contents

War of the Worlds • SIAFU Men's Conference 2012 • Dr. Don L. Davis

Session 1
The Enemy We Fight 3

Session 2
The Equipment We Use 13

Session 3
The Endurance We Display 25

Appendix 39

Bibliography 50

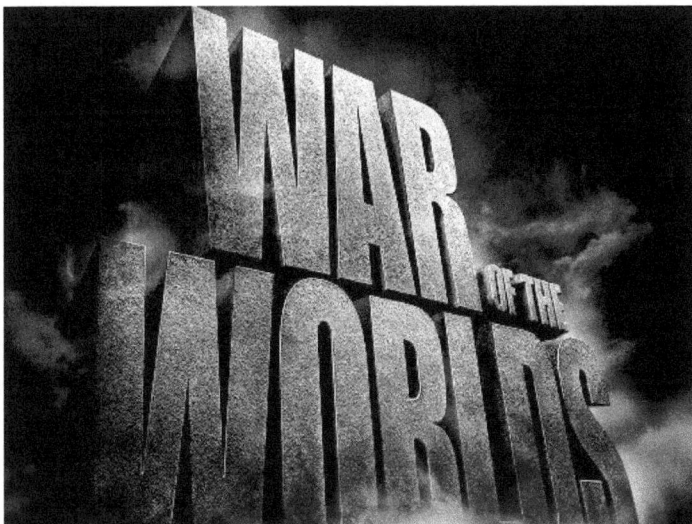

The Enemy We Fight
Ephesians 6.10-12

War of the Worlds
SIAFU Men's Conference 2012
Session 1 • Dr. Don L. Davis

Unless otherwise noted, all Scriptures are taken from the English Standard Version (ESV).

❖❖❖❖❖

The Universe Is At War–Choose A Side

According to the Bible, our lives are lived in the midst of an invisible spiritual war. One of the most dangerous things we can do is simply to ignore this reality. We accept the Bible as true but we often live as though the battle existed on some far-off mission field, not here in our city. The fact is, there is a battle ranging over your city and it is affecting you right now. . . . Every one of us faces demonic forces in our local environment, but as Christians we are called to a bigger battle. We are contending for our whole generation. We are called to act locally but to think globally.

– John Dawson, *Taking Our Cities for God, pp. 27, 29*

The Chain-of-Command of the Cosmos

It was an eye-opening experience for the disciples to discover that "the demons are subject to us in Your name" (Luke 10.17). This verse pictures a group of soldiers snapping to attention and following precisely the orders of their commanding officer. Jesus was telling us that the demons are the soldiers and, in Christ, we are the generals. They must do what we command in Christ's name.

We sometimes mistakenly see God and His kingdom on one side and Satan and his kingdom on the other side. Both kingdoms seem to be very powerful, and here we are, stuck in the middle between the two, like the rope in a tug-of-war. On some days God seems to be winning, and on other days the devil appears to have the upper hand. And we don't seem to have anything to say about who wins the battle.

But that's not how it is. *Spiritual authority is not a tug-of-war; it's a chain of command.* Jesus Christ has all authority in heaven and on earth (Matthew 28.18); He's at the top. He has given His authority and power to His children to be used in His name (Luke 10.17); we're underneath Him. What about Satan and his demons? They're at the bottom, subject to the authority Christ has given to us. They have no more right to rule our lives than an army private has to order a general to clean the latrine.

– Neil T. Anderson and Dave Park, *The Bondage Breaker.* Eugene, OR: Harvest House Publishers, 1993, p. 67-68.

✤✤✤✤✤

As soldiers of the Cross, we enter the war of the worlds, standing strong in the Lord and the strength of his might. We daily strap on the whole armor of God so that we can make a stand against the tricks of the devil. We don't fight against human enemies but against the rulers, against the authorities, against the cosmic powers over this present darkness, and against the spiritual forces of evil in the heavenly realm.

We therefore take up our equipment, the whole armor of God, so that we can resist the enemy's attacks, and, fighting till the end, still hold our ground. So, now, we stand ready, with the belt of truth around our waist, with righteousness as our breastplate, and for shoes the readiness to announce the Gospel of peace.

Above all, we carry the shield of faith, which puts out all the flaming missiles of the evil one. We take the helmet of salvation, and the sword of the Spirit, which is the Word of God.

We endure this struggle by praying on every occasion and in every season in the Spirit. We keep alert and never give up, praying always for all God's people and for Christ's ambassadors in every place. The Holy Spirit empowers us to fight, and leads us into victory, for Jesus' sake.

No weapon formed against us will prosper, for we are more than conquerors through him who loved us. In God alone, we will be powerful in battle, leave no man left behind, and will win the day in this war of the worlds.

— *Inspired by the Hall of Faith of Hebrews 11*

✤✤✤✤✤

I. The Enemy We Fight: Our Struggle Against the Forces of Evil

A. What's the Big Deal?: The Universe Is at War

God declares that, because of sin and rebellion, the entire universe is at war. Since the creation of the universe, a battle has been raging in the heavenlies where God has determined to rescue the universe from the effects of the curse of Satan and the first human pair. Everything is at stake, and not one square inch is not being contested. It is a knock-down, drag-out war for the final control and destiny of creation. It is a battle for preeminence in the universe!

1. The universe is **the Battlefield,** and the earth as **A Central Campaign In the War of the Worlds**

    a. It is a battle that **has been waged since the beginning of time:** *who will ultimately receive honor, worship, and glory as supreme and final Lord in all things?*, Matt. 4.8-10

    b. It is a battle where **everything is affected and involved –the fate of all creation is connected,** Rev. 4.11"Worthy are you, our Lord and God, to receive glory and honor and power, for you created all things, and by your will they existed and were created."

    c. It is a battle where **the stakes are unbelieving high – absolute control and oversight of all creation forever,** 1 Chron. 29.10-12 Therefore David blessed the LORD in the presence of all the assembly. And David said: "Blessed are you, O LORD, the God of Israel our father, forever and ever. [11] Yours, O LORD, is the greatness and the power and the glory and the victory and the majesty, for all that is in the heavens and in the earth is yours. Yours is the kingdom, O LORD, and you are exalted as head above all. [12] Both riches and honor come from you, and you rule over all. In your hand are power and might, and in your hand it is to make great and to give strength to all.

> God the Father is the *Director* of the Story, Jesus of Nazareth is *its Hero and Champion*, the Holy Spirit is *the Narrator and Interpreter* of the Story, and the Scriptures are the *Testimony and Record* of the Story. Everyone is involved and everything is at stake. You must get on the right side of history to survive—and to win!

2. **A cosmic war wages between the LORD and Satan for the control of the universe, v. 10** Repent and believe the Good News of Christ and his Kingdom, Acts 2.38, Mark 1.14-15.

    a. God, the Maker of heaven and earth, is the rightful Owner, Disposer, and Controller of all things, both visible and invisible.

    b. The Lord is sovereign: all things are in his hands, and **the devil is intent on stealing God's rightful authority** from him, Isa. 14.12-15 "How you are fallen from heaven, O Day Star, son of Dawn! How you are cut down to the ground, you who laid the nations low! [13] You said in your heart, 'I will ascend to heaven; above the stars of God I will set my throne on high; I will sit on the mount of assembly in the far reaches of the north; [14] I will ascend above the heights of the clouds; I will make myself like the Most High.' [15] But you are brought down to Sheol, to the far reaches of the pit."

3. The story of Scripture is **the Story of God's determination to save the universe through his Champion, Christus Victor** *(Christ the Victor)*

    a. Through the covenant promise of God, he determined in ages past that he would send to the world a seed who would put down all evil, sin, death, and the devil forever. That seed was *Jesus of Nazareth!*, Mark 1.14-15; Luke 17.

    b. He fulfills God's covenant with *Abraham* (for a Redeemer), Gen. 12.1-3, and with *David* (for a King), Ps. 89; 2 Sam. 7.

c. He is the *Last Adam* (head of a new humanity), Rom. 5, an eternal priest ever interceding for us (Melchizedek), Heb. 7.

d. He inaugurates and brings into being the Reign of God, and will restore all things back under God's rule (Matt. 12.25-30). *In the fullness of time, Christ came inaugurating the Kingdom of God, displaying God's glory and demonstrating his victory over our mortal enemies (sin, death, the grave, the devil), and made the whole creation new!*

Living Out The Story of God:
Anamnesis (You are There) and Prolepsis (Prophetic-Perfect Tense)
Sacred Roots: The Story of God!

B. Hear God's Word: **Combatants in This War of the Worlds**, Eph. 6.10-12

By yourself you don't have the ability to resist Satan and his demons. But *in Christ you do.*
– Neil T. Anderson and Dave Park, *The Bondage Breaker.* Eugene, OR: Harvest House Publishers, 1993, p. 66.

1. **Be strong in the Lord, and in the strength of his might**, v. 10
   Repent and believe the Good News of Christ and his Kingdom, Acts 2.38, Mark 1.14-15.

   a. Through his death and resurrection, he has become the Victor over Hades and death, Rev. 1.17-18.

   b. Jesus is the One whom God chose and anointed as the Messiah, God's champion, who would ultimately defeat the devil, put down sin, and overcome the world, John 16.33; 1 John 5.1-5.

   c. He has defeated our sin nature, and routed the devil's works, shamed and confused his minions, and secured his eternal destruction and defeat, Col. 2.15; 1 John 3.8.

The war in the heavenlies is between the forces of God and the evil one, "who is called the devil and Satan, the deceiver of the whole world" (Rev. 12.9).

- **The devil was the anointed cherub (covering angel)** placed in charge of, or at least offered freedom to roam the newly created earth (Ezek. 28.11-19).
- **The devil (Lucifer, son of the dawn) fell from his high estate** (Isa. 14.9 ff.), and took with him a host of angelic spirits who now make up his army of rulers, principalities and powers (Rev. 12.4ff).
- **Satan is the archenemy of God,** but is not equal with God; he is rather, a rebellious prince of significant strength and resources. He now appears to have access to heaven (Job 1–3), but will be displaced by the forces of God and cast out of heaven (Rev. 12.9ff).
- Scripture provides many descriptions of Satan: he is the **thief** who comes to steal, kill, and destroy (John 10.10), the **deceiver** (2 Cor. 11.3), the **destroyer** (Rev. 9.11, Abaddon means "destroyer"), the **ancient serpent** (Rev. 12), and **devouring lion** (1 Peter 5.8–9).
- The devil, through his control of the world and those who belong to him, is the **"spirit who now works in the sons of disobedience"** (Eph. 2.2, NKJV).
- His **brashness** is extraordinary: he even tempted our Lord, the Christ, Matt. 4.1-11

2. **Put on the whole Armor of God, in order to stand against the schemes of the devil v. 11** The devil is our enemy in this spiritual warfare, 1 Pet. 5.8; Matt. 13.39ff.; Mark 4.15ff.; Luke 8.12; 2 Thess. 3.3

   a. He is the *tempter*, making sin and rebellion look good and profitable, 1 Thess. 3.5; Gen. 3.1-6; Heb. 2.18; 4.15.

   b. He is the *deceiver*, distorting the truth and making worldly lies seem reasonable and acceptable, John 8.44; 2 Cor. 2.11; 4.4; 11.3; Rev. 12.9.

   c. He is the *accuser*, undercutting and undermining believers by accusing them of sin, betrayal, and desertion, Rev. 12.10; Job 1.9-11; Zech. 3.1.

3. Not against flesh and blood: **the enemies we fight are spirit beings, whose leader is Satan, the devil, v. 12**

C. Make It Plain: **The Only Way to Fight Spiritual Enemies Is with Spiritual Weapons.**

Matthew 10.32-33 So everyone who acknowledges me before men, I also will acknowledge before my Father who is in heaven, [33] but whoever denies me before men, I also will deny before my Father who is in heaven.

1. **No Neutrality in This War is Tolerated or Allowed,** Matt. 10.32-33

   a. Repent, believe, and align yourself with Jesus of Nazareth, and prepare to wrestle with the spiritual forces of evil controlling this world, which are hostile to God's truth and God's people.

   b. The world **hates** Christians. *You in this thing, whether you realize it or not!,* John 15.19-20; 1 Pet. 4.12-16.

   c. The world strives to **seduce disciples of Christ** through its lust, greed, and prideful teaching and ways. 1 John 2.15-17; Luke 12.15-19; Titus 2.12; 2 Tim. 4.10; Heb. 11.24-25.

   d. To be a believer is to be a target: Satan **persecutes believers, persecutes the Church, and opposes the Gospel,** Job 2.7; Luke 22.31-32; 2 Tim. 3.12; Rev. 12.13; 2 Cor. 4.4; 1 Pet. 5.8.

2. **Our Enemies are highly trained and dangerous. 1 Peter 5.8**

   a. The Christian soldier must dedicate their lives to **Aggressive Opposition in three the spheres of spiritual warfare: the world, the flesh, and the devil.**

> History is not a meaningless jumble but a controlled pattern, and the Lord Jesus Christ is the One who is directing these events. He is the Lord of history. God is at work in the selfsame events that we look at with such horror and confusion. ~ Ray C. Stedman

b. **Our external enemy: Love not the world,** or any of the things associated with this sinful, rebellious world system, 1 John 2.15-17.

c. **Our internal enemy: Put to death the desires of your sin nature,** and make no provision for your flesh to fulfill its lusts, Col. 3.5; Rom. 13.

d. **Our infernal enemy:** Adopt the stance of a fighter–**resist the devil,** and he will flee from you, James 4.6.

3. We must be aware of **the wiles, strategy, and snares of the devil:** To believe is to *become a warrior of Christ!*

There is much about Satan in the letters of Paul but there is little of direct attack of satanic forces. . . . By far, the majority of attacks of the Devil against Christians are not direct but indirect. That is why they are called the "wiles" of the Devil. Wiliness means deviousness, circuity, something not obvious. We need to examine this more thoroughly, for the major attack of the Devil, and his powers against human life is not by direct means, but indirect–by satanic suggestions through the natural and commonplace events of life.

– Neil T. Anderson and Dave Park, *The Bondage Breaker.*
Eugene, OR: Harvest House Publishers, 1993, p. 46.

a. Learn and apply your knowledge of the devil's wily (read here as "slick") ways, Eph. 6.11.

b. Don't be caught ignorant and unaware of the devil's *devices,* 2 Cor. 2.11.

c. Choose God's side, and stay alert for the presence of *snares, booby-traps, and ambushes* the devil will set for you, Josh. 24.15; 1 Tim. 3.7.

If we are going to made into wine, we will have to be crushed; you cannot drink grapes. ~ Oswald Chambers

Whoever makes a practice of sinning is of the devil, for the devil has been sinning from the beginning. The reason the Son of God appeared was to destroy the works of the devil.

— 1 John 3.8

> **Be broken before the Lord, yielded to his mighty hand,
> and choose this day to serve as a good soldier of Jesus Christ.**

✤✤✤✤✤

You Are A Walking Battlefield:
You Must Be Won Before You Can Win Others

Every Christian is a walking battlefield. Every believer carries deep within himself a terrible conflict. And most of us will gravitate to anything that will help us win the battle. Call it the battle between the flesh and the spirit. Call it the quest for the victorious Christian life. Call it what you want. But it's a flat-out-knock-down-drag-out war. And when it's over, you want to be among those who are still standing. The principles of war are taught in military academies all over the world. In most ways, spiritual warfare is no different than physical warfare. Every soldier who expects to not only survive but win must understand and employ these principles in his own daily battles "against the powers of this dark world and against the spiritual forces of evil in the heavenly realms" (Ephesians 6.12b NIV).

– Stu Webber, *Spirit Warriors*. Sisters, OR: Multnomah Publishers, 2001, p. 16.

✤✤✤✤✤

As soldiers of the Cross, we enter the war of the worlds, standing strong in the Lord and the strength of his might. We daily strap on the whole armor of God so that we can make a stand against the tricks of the devil.

We don't fight against human enemies but against the rulers, against the authorities, against the cosmic powers over this present darkness, and against the spiritual forces of evil in the heavenly realm.

The Bottom Line:_____

The Equipment We Use
Ephesians 6.13-17

War of the Worlds
SIAFU Men's Conference 2012
Session 2 • Dr. Don L. Davis

Unless otherwise noted, all Scriptures are taken from the English Standard Version (ESV).

❖❖❖❖❖

The Great Weapon of the Enemy: Self-Rejection

Over the years, I have come to realize that the greatest trap in our life is not success, popularity, or power, but *self-rejection*. Success, popularity, and power can indeed present a great temptation, but their seductive quality often comes from the way they are part of the much larger temptation to self-rejection. When we have come to believe in the voices that call us worthless and unlovable, then success, popularity, and power are easily perceived as attractive solutions. The real trap, however, is self-rejection. As soon as someone accuses me or criticizes me, as soon as I am rejected, left alone, or abandoned, I find myself thinking, "Well, that proves once again that I am a nobody." ... [My dark side says,] I am no good... I deserve to be pushed aside, forgotten, rejected, and abandoned. Self-rejection is the greatest enemy of the spiritual life because it contradicts the sacred voice that calls us the "Beloved." Being the Beloved constitutes the core truth of our existence. – Henri J. Nouwen

Know Your Enemy, Use Your Weaponry

In battle, a soldier seeks to understand his enemy. If you know what your enemy is like, and what he is apt to do, you can develop a battle plan to defeat him. We as Christians are at war with Satan, but we will never be victorious until we understand the enemy and learn to depend upon our Savior. If we are going to overcome we must adopt a spiritual warfare worldview so that we will have the tools necessary to defeat our enemy. Jesus described Satan this way: "(Satan) was a murderer from the beginning and has always hated the truth. There is no truth in him. When he lies, it is consistent with his character; for he is a liar and the father of lies" (John 8.44).

Jesus warns us that when Satan lies, it is to be expected because it is completely consistent with his character – in other words, lying comes quite naturally to Satan. And not only is he a liar, he is also a murderer. Christians should understand this fact – the devil wants to bring death to you.

He wants to murder your purity, he wants to kill your happiness, he wants to destroy your spiritual life, and he wants nothing more than your death. If you are a Christian, your death takes your influence out of this world. If you are not a Christian, your death delivers you into his evil hands. He will tell any lie, and make up any accusation, in order to kill you.

~ Barry Davis, www.mindofchrist.net

✤✤✤✤✤

As soldiers of the Cross, we enter the war of the worlds, standing strong in the Lord and the strength of his might. We daily strap on the whole armor of God so that we can make a stand against the tricks of the devil. We don't fight against human enemies but against the rulers, against the authorities, against the cosmic powers over this present darkness, and against the spiritual forces of evil in the heavenly realm.

We therefore take up our equipment, the whole armor of God, so that we can resist the enemy's attacks, and, fighting till the end, still hold our ground. So we stand ready, with the belt of truth around our waist, with righteousness as our breastplate, and for shoes the readiness to announce the Gospel of peace.

Above all, we carry the shield of faith, which puts out all the flaming missiles of the evil one. We take the helmet of salvation, and the sword of the Spirit, which is the Word of God.

We endure this struggle by praying on every occasion and in every season in the Spirit. We keep alert and never give up, praying always for all God's people and for Christ's ambassadors in every place. The Holy Spirit empowers us to fight, and leads us into victory, for Jesus' sake.

No weapon formed against us will prosper, for we are more than conquerors through him who loved us. In God alone, we will be powerful in battle, leave no man left behind, and will win the day in this war of the worlds.

— Inspired by the Hall of Faith of Hebrews 11

> **Act like men, be strong in the Lord and the power of his might! Babies sleep a lot; growing leaders listen to the Word of the Lord, regarding their enemies and their equipment to withstand them.**

❖❖❖❖❖

II. The Equipment We Use: Weapons That Bring Down Strongholds in Jesus' Name

A. What's the Big Deal?: God Has Provided Supernatural Weapons for the Fight, 2 Cor. 10.3-5

2 Corinthians 10.3-5 For though we walk in the flesh, we are not waging war according to the flesh. [4] For the weapons of our warfare are not of the flesh but have divine power to destroy strongholds. [5] We destroy arguments and every lofty opinion raised against the knowledge of God, and take every thought captive to obey Christ,

Our problem is that we have become so accustomed to believing our feelings as though they were facts. We never examine them. We never take them and look at them and ask, "Is this true?" We simply say, "I feel this way. Therefore it must be true." This is why so many are constantly defeated; they accept their feelings as facts. Rather, we are to say, "Christ is my righteousness. I am linked with him. I am one with him. His life is my life and my life is his life. We are married. Therefore, I cannot believe this lie that these evil thoughts are my thoughts. They are not my thoughts at all. They are thoughts which come because of another force. It is not my thinking at all. No, it is the Devil again. I do not want these thoughts. I do not like them. I reject them. I do not want them in my thinking; therefore they are not mine. They are the Devil's children, and I'll spank them and send them back where they belong!"

– Ray Stedman, Spiritual Warfare: Waco, TX: Word Books, 1976, p. 129.

1. The *nature of the* **Battle** demands *supernatural weapons and equipment:* the **Battle occurs in the realm of the spirit**

    a. God is the commander of an army of soldiers, Ps. 89.8 O LORD God of hosts, who is mighty as you are, O LORD, with your faithfulness all around you? (The term here translated "LORD God of hosts" can be translated "LORD God of armies," cf. 1 Kings 19.10; Jer. 5.14; Hos. 12.5; Amos 4.13)

b.   The spirit realm is where the work of spiritual warfare takes place, in the mind, the soul, and the spirit, the armor of light, Rom. 13.12 The night is far gone; the day is at hand. So then let us cast off the works of darkness and put on the armor of light.

2.   The *nature of the* **Enemy** demands *supernatural weapons and equipment:* **the enemies in the spirit realm are cunning, persistent, and deadly**

a.   The enemies in the spirit real are **Cunning:** *the sons of Sceva,* Acts 19.11-20, cf. Acts 19.15 But the evil spirit answered them, "Jesus I know, and Paul I recognize, but who are you?"

b.   The enemies in the spirit real are **Persistent:** *looking for the "opportune time,"* Matthew 4.8-10; Luke 4.1-13, cf. Luke 4.13 And when the devil had ended every temptation, he departed from him until an opportune time.

c.   The enemies in the spirit real are **Deadly:** *looks to sift believers like wheat,* Luke 22.31-32"Simon, Simon, behold, Satan demanded to have you, that he might sift you like wheat, [32] but I have prayed for you that your faith may not fail. And when you have turned again, strengthen your brothers." Matthew 4.8-10

3.   The *nature of our* **Weakness** demands *supernatural weapons and equipment:* **God's will and authority are constantly being contested in our lives**

a.   We are to **arm ourselves with the same thinking** as our Lord, 1 Peter 4.1-2 Since therefore Christ suffered in the flesh, arm yourselves with the same way of thinking, for whoever has suffered in the flesh has ceased from sin, [2] so as to live for the rest of the time in the flesh no longer for human passions but for the will of God.

b. Spiritual warfare allows us to **Withstand the Devil's lies and attacks,** and to remain faithful to God in our walk before him, Romans 13.12-14 The night is far gone; the day is at hand. So then let us cast off the works of darkness and put on the armor of light. [13] Let us walk properly as in the daytime, not in orgies and drunkenness, not in sexual immorality and sensuality, not in quarreling and jealousy. [14] But put on the Lord Jesus Christ, and make no provision for the flesh, to gratify its desires.

> We hear a great deal about night life. The believer is identified with day life. He walks as one who belongs to the day. ~ J. Vernon McGee

B. Hear God's Word: **Strap on the Full Armor of God, Eph. 6.13-17**

The whole armor of God, which he has provided to you through Jesus Christ the Lord, is sufficient for you to do battle in the name of the Lord. Giving amazing power to function both offensively and defensively, you must every day put it on prayerfully, and use it faithfully. In doing so you will repel every attack of the enemy.

1. **Take up the whole armor of God that you may be able to withstand against the schemes of the devil, v. 13**

   a. We need the *whole armor of God,* (each piece is critical and necessary), 1 Thess. 5.8-10 But since we belong to the day, let us be sober, having put on the breastplate of faith and love, and for a helmet the hope of salvation. [9] For God has not destined us for wrath, but to obtain salvation through our Lord Jesus Christ, [10] who died for us so that whether we are awake or asleep we might live with him, Matt. 28.18-20.

b.   No believer is immune from the fight: *the enemies of God most certainly will engage and seek to destroy the Christian, whenever and however they can* (including mentally, physically, spiritually, relationally, and professionally), 2 Tim. 3.12

  (1) Opposed the first believers in persecution, Acts 6.8-14; 7.54-58
  (2) Stephen stoned to death, Acts 7.54-58
  (3) Saul causing havoc with believers in Jerusalem, Acts 8.1-3
  (4) Violent, vicious hostility toward Paul and the brothers, Acts 9.23; 14.5,19; 16.16-24; 17.5-6, etc.
  (5) Plots and plans to destroy God's workers, Acts 23.12-15; 25.3

c.   This weaponry is most needed in *the "evil day,"* i.e., when the battle is fiercest and most vulnerable, e.g., Jesus in the wilderness, Matt. 4.1-11.

2.   Stand, fastening to your side **the belt of Truth, v. 14a.** Believers must *possess a strong biblical understanding of God's truth* and will, which can counter *Satan's deception and deceit,* Ps. 119.95, 116; Eph. 4.14-15; Col. 2.6-8; 2 Tim. 1.13-14; John 8.31-32 So Jesus said to the Jews who had believed in him, "If you abide in my word, you are truly my disciples, [32] and you will know the truth, and the truth will set you free."

3.   Put on **the Breastplate of Righteousness, v. 14b.** Believers must be assured that they are *righteous in God's sight through Christ,* which can counter *Satan's accusations,* 2 Cor. 5.18-21; Isa. 61.10; Phil. 3.7-9

4.   Lace up **for shoes the readiness to announce the Gospel of Peace, v. 15.** Believers must *cling to the Good News,* which can counter *Satan's use of fear* in troubled times, John 14.27; 16.33; Phil. 4.6-7 do not be anxious about anything, but in everything by prayer and supplication with thanksgiving let your requests be made known to God. [7] And the peace of God, which surpasses all understanding, will guard your hearts and your minds in Christ Jesus.

> As a Christian, if you don't believe you have authority, you're not going to exercise it. If your belief is weak, your expression of it will also be weak and ineffective. But if you have a confident grip on the authority that Christ has given you, you will exercise it with confidence. ~ Neal Anderson and Dave Park

5. In all circumstances **take up the Shield of Faith, v. 16.** Believers must exercising *faith and dependence on God and his Word,* which can counter *Satan's intimidation, doubt, and false sense of being overwhelmed,* Rom. 1.17; Hab. 2.4; 1 Pet. 5.8-9; 1 John 5.1-5; 1 Timothy 6.11-12 But as for you, O man of God, flee these things. Pursue righteousness, godliness, faith, love, steadfastness, gentleness. [12] Fight the good fight of the faith. Take hold of the eternal life to which you were called and about which you made the good confession in the presence of many witnesses.

6. Take up **the Helmet of Salvation, v. 17.** Believers must stir up *expectations of future glory,* which can *counter Satan's effort to generate despair* about the future, 1 Thess. 5.8-9; Titus 2.11-14; 1 John 3.3

7. Wield with skill **the Sword of the Spirit (the Word of God), v. 17b.** Believers must learn *skillful use of the Word of God,* which can counter *Satan's lies, falsehoods, and distortions,* Ps. 119.9-11; 2 Tim. 3.16-17; Heb. 4.12-13.

C. Make It Plain: **Equip yourself to employ the Full Armor of God with skill and effectiveness**

Those who are responding to the authority of Christ will both recognize and respond to those leaders that he has placed in their lives for direction, oversight, and protection.

1. Publicly **join and live faithfully within a platoon of the Lord** (i.e., a local church), and **report to your commanders** for *duty* (local pastors and leaders), Heb. 10.24-25.

a.   Believers, from the beginning, have met weekly for the Word and sacrament, e.g., Acts 20.7.

b.   We come together to offer spiritual sacrifices acceptable to God through Jesus Christ, and to build one another up in our faith, 1 Pet. 2.3-4; 1 Cor. 14.23.

c.   We need the ongoing support, instruction, and protection of a local church like individual members of the body needs the entire body for survival, Rom. 12.4-8; Eph. 4.9-15; 1 Cor. 12.1-27; 1 Peter 4.9-10

2.   Strap **the heavenly armor on daily, and use it constantly to develop your skill in using it**

a.   Get your act together: **discipline yourself** so you may represent your captain well (e.g., prayer, fasting, study, Scripture memorization, meditation, worship, solitude, etc.), 1 Tim. 4.7-10.

b.   Number your days: *redeem the time*, Ps. 90.10-12; Eph. 5.15-17.

c.   Discipline your body: *get you appetites under control (including sleep, hunger, sexuality, and your exercise)*, 1 Cor. 9.24-27.

d.   Pay careful attention to your thought life: *don't be ruled by habits of lust, anger, and pride*, Phil. 4.8.

e.   Get a grip on the way you spend money, Matt. 6.24.

f.   Control your tongue: *banish whining, backbiting, blameshifting, complaining, and excuses as cowardly and unchristian*, Phil. 2.14-16; James 3.1-5.

Soldiers must learn how to use the weapons of the Lord gradually over time through faithful practice (**incrementalism**) and in the midst of situations where struggle and difficulty are happening (**privation**), 2 Tim. 2.1-2

- **Start small, don't quit:** expect difficulty, misery, and tribulation, and be prepared to go through, not around, Gal. 6.7-9.
- **Bear all things:** don't allow excuses to hide a lack of discipline, 1 Cor. 13.7; 2 Tim. 3.12; Acts 14.22.
- **Don't be ashamed to suffer:** resistance of the enemy involves struggle which is the key to achievement, 2 Tim. 1.8; James 4.7; 1 Pet. 5.8-9.
- **Endure all for the sake of God's people:** the more you learn to suffer, the better you learn to serve, 2 Tim. 2.10.
- **Take courage from Jesus' example:** he endured much for the sake of triumph that awaited him, Heb. 12.1-3 , John 16.33; 15.20-21.

---

3. Befriend and submit to **experienced soldiers who can equip you to fight**.

   a. Learn the art of joyful obedience to your commanders, Heb. 13.17 Obey your leaders and submit to them, for they are keeping watch over your souls, as those who will have to give an account. Let them do this with joy and not with groaning, for that would be of no advantage to you.

   b. Ask God to bring you a mentor, a seasoned officer whom you can learn from and submit to, 2 Tim. 2.2 *beware of pride, grumbling, and backbiting leadership,* Isa. 14.12-17; Num. 14.2-4.

   c. Remember, the armor of God is for the purpose of withstanding in the evil day: *it works best when you need it most!*

I love you, O LORD, my strength. [2] The LORD is my rock and my fortress and my deliverer, my God, my rock, in whom I take refuge, my shield, and the horn of my salvation, my stronghold. [3] I call upon the LORD, who is worthy to be praised, and I am saved from my enemies. – *Psalms 18.1-3*

> The armor that God has provided cannot yield ins power in the hands of an undisciplined, unyielded soldier. His equipment s will prove less valuable if you fail to surrender to the Lord without qualification or condition. As the Father sent our Lord into the world, so we now, in the places where we live and work, have been sent into our worlds to represent the Christ and his Kingdom.

✠✠✠✠✠

You Have Been Born into the Middle of the "Mother of All Battles"

They say "Old Blood 'n' Guts" George Patton was born in the middle of a battlefield. He was meant to be a soldier. And so were you. In fact, we have it on good authority—the Word of God—that every one of us was born in the midst of "the mother of all battles."

The war started long before you were born. It began a long time ago in a century far, far away, at the beginning of time as we know it. About the time when the earth was formless and void and darkness was over the face of the deep. Sometime, somewhere in eternity past, a powerful angelic being named Lucifer challenged the rule of almighty God. Prior to those opening salvos, God's universe had known only peace and harmony. Not so much as a shadow of war.

Before that opening challenge, there was only God and His angels. Together. In perfect peace. There was no division, no separation, no pain, no confusion, no anxiety, and no death. But the head angel, Lucifer himself, decided it was time to make a move. To move on up. To assert himself, so to speak. The fall of Satan (Lucifer's alias, which means "adversary") was sparked by our old nemesis, pride. It was the old "I'll do it my way" lie.

Right in the middle of this cosmic "mother of all battles" between God and Satan, planet earth was birthed: a bright, blue-and-white marble spinning in the black velvet of space. And the capstone of creation on that little planet was humankind, male and female. That's you and me. That's men and women, boys and girls. Born for battle. Weaned for war. Meant to be soldiers.

You see, the earth was created to be a model, a microcosm, a king demonstrating to a watching universe what life under the rule of God was like. It was a kingdom worth defending. God accepted Satan's challenge and decided to let the battle run its course for a bit. All the earth is a stage, a giant arena for battle, the ultimate fight site. Numberless angels fill the seats awaiting the outcome. You and I are on the battlefield, right at the point of action.

— Stu Webber, Spirit Warriors. Sisters, OR: Multnomah Publishers, 2001, pp. 22-23.

✛✛✛✛✛

We therefore take up our equipment, the whole armor of God, so that we can resist the enemy's attacks, and, fighting till the end, still hold our ground. So we stand ready, with the belt of truth around our waist, with righteousness as our breastplate, and for shoes the readiness to announce the Gospel of peace.

Above all, we carry the shield of faith, which puts out all the flaming missiles of the evil one. We take the helmet of salvation, and the sword of the Spirit, which is the Word of God.

The Bottom Line:_____

The Endurance We Display
Ephesians 6.18-20

War of the Worlds
SIAFU Men's Conference 2012
Session 3 • Dr. Don L. Davis

Unless otherwise noted, all Scriptures are taken from the English Standard Version (ESV).

✢✢✢✢✢

Prayer Is a Wartime Walkie-Talkie

In wartime, prayer takes on a different significance. It becomes a wartime walkie-talkie and no longer a domestic intercom. Jesus said to his disciples, "You did not choose me, but I chose you, and appointed you, that you should go and bear fruit, and that your fruit should remain, in order that whatever you ask of the Father in my name, he may give to you" (John 15.16).

Notice the amazing logic of this verse. He gave them a mission "in order that" the Father would have prayers to answer. This means that prayer is for mission. It is designed to advance the kingdom. That's why the Lord's Prayer begins by asking God to see to it that his name be hallowed and that his kingdom come.

James warned about the misuse of prayer as a domestic intercom to call the butler for another pillow. He said, "You do not have because you do not ask. You ask and do not receive, because you ask with wrong motives, so that you may spend it on your pleasures" (James 4.2-3).

Prayer is always kingdom oriented. Even when we pray for healing and for help, it is that the kingdom purposes of God in the world may advance. Otherwise we have turned a wartime walkie-talkie into a domestic intercom.

Let us pray with the apostle Paul, "that the word of the Lord may spread rapidly and be glorified" (2 Thessalonians 3.1)."

– The Desiring God Resource Library, "Driving Convictions Behind Foreign Missions,"
January 1, 1996, By John Piper and Tom Steller

Falling and Rising as a Christian Soldier

In our churches we often sing, "Arise, my soul, arise! Shake off thy guilty fears." But nothing happens and we keep our fears. Why do we claim on one hand that our sins are gone and on the other act just as though they are not gone?

Brethren, we have been declared "Not Guilty!" by the highest court in all the universe. Still there are honest Christians, earnestly seeking the face of God, who cannot seem to break loose and find real freedom. The grave clothes trip them up every time they try to move on a little faster. Satan uses their past sins to terrify them.

Now, on the basis of grace as taught in the Word of God, when God forgives a man, He trusts him as though he had never sinned. God did not have mental reservations about any of us when we became His children by faith. When God forgives a man, He doesn't think, I will have to watch this fellow because he has a bad record. No, He starts with him again as though he had just been created and as if there had been no past at all! That is the basis of our Christian assurance—and God wants us to be happy in it.

— A. W. Tozer on Christian Leadership, wordsearchbible, Electronic Edition, 2012, p. 288.

✢✢✢✢✢

As soldiers of the Cross, we enter the war of the worlds, standing strong in the Lord and the strength of his might. We daily strap on the whole armor of God so that we can make a stand against the tricks of the devil. We don't fight against human enemies but against the rulers, against the authorities, against the cosmic powers over this present darkness, and against the spiritual forces of evil in the heavenly realm.

We therefore take up our equipment, the whole armor of God, so that we can resist the enemy's attacks, and, fighting till the end, still hold our ground. So we stand ready, with the belt of truth around our waist, with righteousness as our breastplate, and for shoes the readiness to announce the Gospel of peace.

Above all, we carry the shield of faith, which puts out all the flaming missiles of the evil one. We take the helmet of salvation, and the sword of the Spirit, which is the Word of God.

We endure this struggle by praying on every occasion and in every season in the Spirit. We keep alert and never give up, praying always for all God's people and for Christ's ambassadors in every place. The Holy Spirit empowers us to fight, and leads us into victory, for Jesus' sake.

No weapon formed against us will prosper, for we are more than conquerors through him who loved us. In God alone, we will be powerful in battle, leave no man left behind, and will win the day in this war of the worlds.

— Inspired by the Hall of Faith of Hebrews 11

✥✥✥✥✥

III. The Endurance We Display: Refusing to Shrink Back from the Hardness of the Fight

A. What's the Big Deal?: Every Christian Soldier Is Tempted to Give Up, to Give In to Fear and Doubt.

Hebrews 3.12-14 Take care, brothers, lest there be in any of you an evil, unbelieving heart, leading you to fall away from the living God. [13] But exhort one another every day, as long as it is called "today," that none of you may be hardened by the deceitfulness of sin. [14] For we have come to share in Christ, if indeed we hold our original confidence firm to the end.

1. The world is **Relentless: 24/7 meddlin' and hasslin'**

   a. Temptations **never take a break,** 1 Cor. 10.12-13 Therefore let anyone who thinks that he stands take heed lest he fall. [13] No temptation has overtaken you that is not common to man. God is faithful, and he will not let you be tempted beyond your ability, but with the temptation he will also provide the way of escape, that you may be able to endure it.

b. Satan entices, making **sin look good,** Gen. 3.4-6 But the serpent said to the woman, "You will not surely die. [5] For God knows that when you eat of it your eyes will be opened, and you will be like God, knowing good and evil." [6] So when the woman saw that the tree was good for food, and that it was a delight to the eyes, and that the tree was to be desired to make one wise, she took of its fruit and ate, and she also gave some to her husband who was with her, and he ate.

c. Like holy men of old, we are **constantly bombarded with the urge to compromise,** James 5.10-11 As an example of suffering and patience, brothers, take the prophets who spoke in the name of the Lord. [11] Behold, we consider those blessed who remained steadfast. You have heard of the steadfastness of Job, and you have seen the purpose of the Lord, how the Lord is compassionate and merciful.

2. The flesh is **Unyielding: the Sin Nature Resists the Spirit's Leading.**

a. The Christian life is a constant, unbroken struggle against temptation and the nature of sin, Heb. 3.13; Acts 20.28; Rom. 7.14-25.

b. Even when you desire to do good, your sin nature will try to drag you down into sin, Rom. 7.14-25.

c. Soldiers of Christ must strive to exchange our fleshly desire for righteous behavior, Rom. 1312-14 ("taking off" old lifestyles and "putting on" new ones through the Spirit's power, see also Eph. 4.22-24; Col. 3.7-10; 1 Tim. 6.11; 2 Tim. 2.22)

3. The devil is **determined: the Enemy roams about seeking someone to devour, 1 Pet. 5.8-9.**

B.   Hear God's Word: **Sustained personal and corporate Prayer produces endurance, Eph. 6.18-20**

But we are not alone in this battle—this conflict with doubt, dismay, fear, confusion and uncertainty. No, there are others around us who are weaker and younger in Christ than we are, and there are still others who are stronger than we. But all of us are all fighting this battle together.

We cannot put on the armor of God for another person, but we can pray for that other person. We can call in reinforcements when we find him engaged in a struggle greater than he can handle for the moment, or perhaps for which he is not fully equipped. It may be, you see, that he has not yet learned how to handle his armor adequately. We are to be aware of other people's problems and pray for them. We are to pray that their eyes will be open to danger, and we are to help them realize how much is available in the armor God has given them, for it is a means of specific help and strength for specific trial. – Ray Stedman, *Spiritual Warfare:* Waco, TX: Word Books, 1976, p. 129.

1.   The warrior of God must **Pray at all times in the Spirit, with all perseverance and petition, v. 18a**

a.   Spiritual warfare demands constant, unbroken, believing prayer, cf. Luke 18.1-17, Luke 18.1 And he told them a parable to the effect that they ought always to pray and not lose heart.

b.   Persistence in prayer gets us what we need, Luke 11.5-10, see vv. 9-10. [9] And I tell you, ask, and it will be given to you; seek, and you will find; knock, and it will be opened to you. [10] For everyone who asks receives, and the one who seeks finds, and to the one who knocks it will be opened.

c.   We must learn the art of "flash prayer" (Frank Laubach), 1 Thess. 5.17 Pray without ceasing

2.   The warrior of God must **never lose sight of the fight, staying alert and praying for all saints who do battle, v. 18b.**

a.   Praying at *all times:* **committed to prayer as constant habit**

b.   With *all prayer and supplication:* **seeking God in adoration, confession, intercession, praise, blessing**

c.   With *all perseverance:* **a non-stop-won't-quit kind of prayer**

d.   Making supplication for *all the saints:* **using it to call down blessing on the People of God everywhere**

God's warrior must cultivate patience in the face of adversity, persecution, setback, and discouragement.

Patience is an active endurance of opposition, not a passive resignation. Patience and patient are used to translate several Hebrew and Greek words. Patience is endurance, steadfastness, long suffering, and forbearance.

God is patient (Rom. 15.5). He is slow to anger in relation to the Hebrews (Exod. 34.6; Num. 14.18, Neh. 9.17; Ps. 86.15; Isa. 48.9; Hos. 11.8-9). The Hebrews were frequently rebellious, but God patiently dealt with them. Jesus' parable of the tenants depicted God's patience with His people (Mark 12.1-11). God's patience with sinners allows time for them to repent (Rom. 2.4), especially in the apparent delay of the return of Christ (2 Pet. 3.9-10).

God's people are to be patient. The psalmist learned to be patient when confronted with the prosperity of the wicked (Ps. 37.1-3,9-13,34-38). Christians should face adversity patiently (Rom. 5.3-5). Patience is a fruit of the Spirit (Gal. 5.22). Christian love is patient (1 Cor. 13.4,7). Ministers are to be patient (2 Cor. 6.6).

Christians need patient endurance in the face of persecution. Hebrews stressed endurance as the alternative to shrinking back during adversity (Heb. 6.9-15; 10.32-39). Jesus is the great example of endurance (Heb. 12.1-3). Perseverance is part of maturity (Jas. 1.2-4). Job's perseverance is another example for suffering Christians (Jas. 5.11). John frequently highlighted the patient endurance of Christians (Rev. 2.2,19; 3.10; 13.10; 14.12). Christian patience is ultimately a gift from God (Rom. 15.5-6; 2 Thess. 3.5). ~ Warren Williams, "Patience" in *Holman Bible Dictionary,* elec. ed. 2012.

---

3.   The warrior of God must **Pray for those who serve and suffer as ambassadors of the Kingdom, v. 19-20.**

C.   Make It Plain: **Prayer is the walkie-talkie of God's Platoon, calling down pin-point grace from Headquarters during the Fight.**

Ps 55.16–19 But I call to God, and the LORD will save me. [17] Evening and morning and at noon I utter my complaint and moan, and he hears my voice. [18] He redeems my soul in safety from the battle that I wage, for many are arrayed against me. [19] God will give ear and humble them, he who is enthroned from of old, Selah, because they do not change and do not fear God.

1.   Moses, with **Aaron and Hur on the mount,** Exod. 17.8-13, Exod. 17.12-13 But Moses' hands grew weary, so they took a stone and put it under him, and he sat on it, while Aaron and Hur held up his hands, one on one side, and the other on the other side. So his hands were steady until the going down of the sun. [13] And Joshua overwhelmed Amalek and his people with the sword.

2.   Elijah on **Mount Carmel with the priests of Baal**, 1 Kings 18.36-38 And at the time of the offering of the oblation, Elijah the prophet came near and said, "O LORD, God of Abraham, Isaac, and Israel, let it be known this day that you are God in Israel, and that I am your servant, and that I have done all these things at your word. [37] Answer me, O LORD, answer me, that this people may know that you, O LORD, are God, and that you have turned their hearts back." [38] Then the fire of the LORD fell and consumed the burnt offering and the wood and the stones and the dust, and licked up the water that was in the trench. There is no middle ground, Josh. 24.15.

Armor and weapons are not sufficient to win a battle; there must be **energy** to do the job. Our energy comes from prayer. We use the sword of the Spirit, and we pray in the Spirit: the Holy Spirit empowers us to win the battle. Read again Eph. 3.14–21 and dare to believe it. The Word of God and prayer are the two resources God has given the church to overcome the enemy and gain territory for God's glory. Note Acts 20.32 and Acts 6.4; also 1 Sam. 12.23. Christian soldiers must pray with their eyes open. "Watch and pray" is God's secret for overcoming the world (Mark 13.33), the flesh (Mark 14.38), and the devil (Eph. 6.18). We should also "watch and pray" for opportunities to serve Christ (Col. 4.2–3). ~ Warren Wiersbe

3. Daniel in exile, **Praying on behalf of Fallen Jerusalem,** Dan. 9.1-23, cf. v. 23 Dan. 9.22-23 He made me understand, speaking with me and saying, "O Daniel, I have now come out to give you insight and understanding. [23] At the beginning of your pleas for mercy a word went out, and I have come to tell it to you, for you are greatly loved. Therefore consider the word and understand the vision."

4. Jesus our Lord in **the Garden of Gethsemane,** Luke 22.39-46

D. Warriors of the City for Christ: **The Siafu Network**

Mission statment: The SIAFU Network is a national association of chapters anchored in local urban churches specifically designed to identify, equip, and release spiritually qualified servant leaders to reach and transform the poorest, unreached communities in urban America.

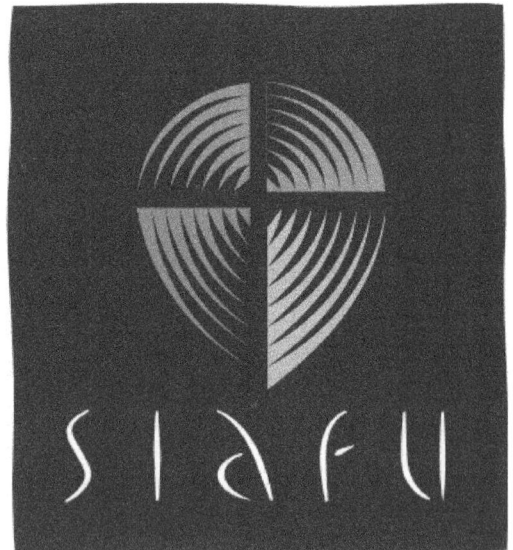

The proposed mission of the Siafu (pronounced see-AH-foo) Network is to establish a viable, effective network of urban Christian men and women whose goal is to inspire each other to take full responsibility for one another's lives and well-being. As soldiers of Christ, we desire to stand for our marriages and families, for our churches and congregations, and for our communities to advance the Kingdom of Christ in the city. Our desire will be to empower urban Christians to both befriend and mentor one another in order to equip each other to evangelize our unchurched family members and friends, to follow-up and disciple new Christians to live the Christian life, and to serve as faithful stewards and servants in our respective Christian churches as outposts of the Kingdom where God has placed them. We also hope to collaborate together in order to identify, train, and release godly, spiritually qualified laborers who can plant churches and help spawn church planting movements which will target the unreached urban neighborhoods of America.

1. Gatherings where we **Encourage and Inspire,** Rom. 15.4-7 whatever was written in former days was written for our instruction, that through endurance and through the encouragement of the Scriptures we might have

hope. [5] May the God of endurance and encouragement grant you to live in such harmony with one another, in accord with Christ Jesus, [6] that together you may with one voice glorify the God and Father of our Lord Jesus Christ. [7] Therefore welcome one another as Christ has welcomed you, for the glory of God.

2. Chapters where we **Challenge and Exhort**, Heb. 10.24-25 And let us consider how to stir up one another to love and good works, [25] not neglecting to meet together, as is the habit of some, but encouraging one another, and all the more as you see the Day drawing near.

3. Projects where we **Collaborate and Serve**, Phil. 1.27 Only let your manner of life be worthy of the gospel of Christ, so that whether I come and see you or am absent, I may hear of you that you are standing firm in one spirit, with one mind striving side by side for the faith of the gospel

> Colossians 4.2-4 (ESV) 2 Continue steadfastly in prayer, being watchful in it with thanksgiving. 3 At the same time, pray also for us, that God may open to us a door for the word, to declare the mystery of Christ, on account of which I am in prison— 4 that I may make it clear, which is how I ought to speak.

I charge you in the presence of God, who gives life to all things, and of Christ Jesus, who in his testimony before Pontius Pilate made the good confession, [14] to keep the commandment unstained and free from reproach until the appearing of our Lord Jesus Christ, [15] which he will display at the proper time—he who is the blessed and only Sovereign, the King of kings and Lord of lords, [16] who alone has immortality, who dwells in unapproachable light, whom no one has ever seen or can see. To him be honor and eternal dominion. Amen.

— 1 Timothy 4.13-16

✥✥✥✥✥

You Are on the Battlefield–Call Down Fire When and Where You Need It

I have been impressed more than ever before that God has given us prayer not as an intercom for increased convenience in our secluded cottages, but as a walkie-talkie connecting the general's headquarters with the transportation line and the field hospital and the front line artillery. Prayer is not a bell to call the servants to satisfy some desire we happen to feel, it is a battlefield transmitter for staying in touch with the general.

– John Piper, Sermon on Ephesians 6, "The Weapon Serves the Wielding Power."

We endure this struggle by praying on every occasion and in every season in the Spirit. We keep alert and never give up, praying always for all God's people and for Christ's ambassadors in every place.

✣✣✣✣✣

The Bottom Line:_____

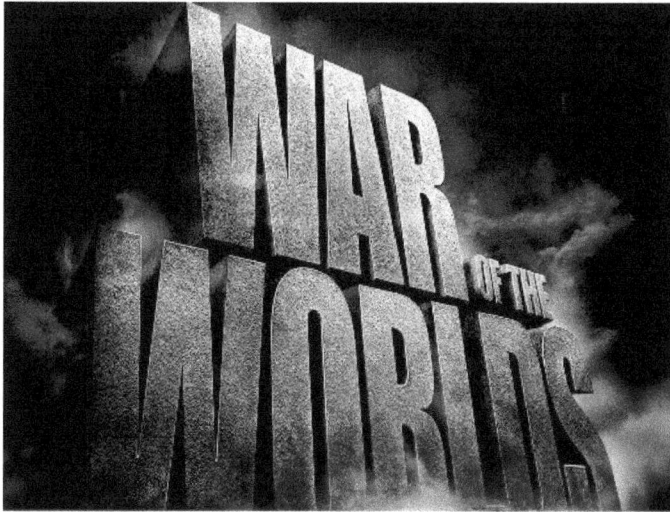

Last Words:
A Parting Challenge
Ephesians 1.13; 5.18; 6.18

Unless otherwise noted, all Scriptures are taken from the English Standard Version (ESV).

❖❖❖❖❖

IV. Go Forth Into Battle In the Name of the Lord: Last Words

A. SIAFU: Arm yourself with a mind to fight, Nehemiah 4.14

And I looked and arose and said to the nobles and to the officials and to the rest of the people, "Do not be afraid of them. Remember the Lord, who is great and awesome, and fight for your brothers, your sons, your daughters, your wives, and your homes."

1. Clean house (& barn): don't play around; end the foolishness today
2. Join a platoon: become a member, not an attender
3. Submit to an officer: come under pastoral care and authority
4. Recite the code daily: start a daily discipline
5. Organize a unit: cell groups allow for maximum support
6. Endure hardness: expect things to get tough
7. Stand your ground: don't give in after difficulty
8. Win your circle: concentrate on winning your folk close-by
9. For resources: www.tumi.org/siafu

A Spirit-controlled Christian has a true, godly sense of courage and boldness in spiritual warfare. Just before entering the Promised Land, Joshua was challenged four times to be strong and courageous (Joshua 1.6,7,9,18). When the early church prayed about their mission of sharing the gospel in Jerusalem, "the place where they had gathered together

was shaken, and they were all filled with the Holy Spirit, and began to speak the word of God with boldness" (Acts 4.31). Spirit-inspired boldness is behind every successful advance in the church today.
— Neil T. Anderson and Dave Park, *The Bondage Breaker.* Eugene, OR: Harvest House Publishers, 1993, p. 73.

B. Burn all bridges leading to compromise: Choose a side, and stick with it, Deut. 30.11-20

I call heaven and earth to witness against you today, that I have set before you life and death, blessing and curse. Therefore choose life, that you and your offspring may live, loving the Lord your God, obeying his voice and holding fast to him, for he is your life and length of days, that you may dwell in the land that the Lord swore to your fathers, to Abraham, to Isaac, and to Jacob, to give them. ~ Deut. 30.19-20

Truth and obedience are key issues in living a Christ-dependent lifestyle. But truth can only be believed if it is understood, and commandments can only be obeyed if they are known. As the Holy Spirit leads us into all truth, we must respond by trusting and obeying: "The one who says, 'I have come to know Him,' and does not keep his commandments, is a liar and the truth is not in him" (1 John 2.4). Disobedience allows Satan to work in us.
— Neil T. Anderson, *Released from Bondage.* San Bernandino, CA: Here's Life Publishers, 1991, p. 38-39.

C. Never give in to evil: Fight like crazy, and expect to be pushed to your limit, especially in the evil day, Eph. 6.10-13

In spiritual warfare the battle is not yours. Even after all is said and done, the ultimate victory is in the hand of the Lord who, through his sovereign purpose, has given us the victory in Jesus Christ. The Holy Spirit lives within us to make this victory real, and apply it to all areas of our lives. We need only yield to him to experience its continuous power and blessing.

1. Don't be bullied by evil
2. Push back
3. Hook up with a tight group that knows how to represent

The War of the Worlds: Three E's of Spiritual Warfare, Eph. 6.10-20
Rev. Dr. Don L. Davis, Page 37

D. Step out front: **Though we appear out-numbered, out-gunned, and out-manned, we will win the day, 2 Chron. 20.1-12.**

Never be afraid to stand on the promises of God. His word is true, his Spirit is real, and his victory is certain. Christ is the Victor over the powers of the curse, hell, death, and the grave. We can take our cities for God, for Jesus is Lord!

At the moment of conversion, all of God's resources are available to us. Unfortunately, nobody pushes the "clear" button in our previously programmed minds. Until God's transformation process begins in our lives, we live in a state of being conformed to this world and regimented by it. That's why Paul writes, "Do not conform any longer to the pattern of this world, but be transformed by the renewing of your mind. Then you will be able to test and approve what God's will is—His good, pleasing and perfect will" (Rom. 12.2, N IV). Therefore-

- the major task of Christian education is to disciple previously programmed people, living independent of God, into a dependant relationship with Him.

- the major task of discipleship/counseling is to free people from their past and eradicate old defense mechanisms by substituting Christ as their only defense.
  – Neil T. Anderson, *Released from Bondage.* San Bernandino, CA: Here's Life Publishers, 1991, p. 38.

Not by Power, Nor Might, but by the Holy Spirit

We are empowered as we hourly, daily depend on the leading and power of the Holy Spirit. It is impossible to be a soldier of Christ and win in spiritual battle apart from his leading and gifts.

- **The Holy Spirit forms and dwells within God's people the church:** 1Cor. 12.13; See also Acts 2.1-4,16-18; Joel 2.28-29; Acts 10.44-48; Eph. 2.21-22; 1 Cor. 3.16; 6.19; John 16.14
- **The Holy Spirit provides power and gifts to the body of Christ:** 1Cor. 12.7 see also Exod. 31.1-5; Num. 11.24-27; 1Sam.10.5-11; Rom. 12.5; 1 Cor. 12.8-11
- **The Holy Spirit enables Christian unity, empowering us to worship, serve, and speak in his power and leading:** Worship: Acts 2.11; John 4.24; Acts 10.45-46; Phil. 3.3; Serve: Rom. 12.6-8; 1 Cor. 12. 7-11; Eph. 4.7-13; Speak: Acts 6.10; 1 Cor. 2.9-16; 14.24-25
- **The Holy Spirit empowers us to bear witness to Jesus to our family and friends, associates and neighbors, and those in our life circle:** Acts 1.8; John 15.26-27; 20.21-23;

The Last Word: _____

Appendix

War of the Worlds • SIAFU Men's Conference 2012 • Dr. Don L. Davis

The Story of God: Our Sacred Roots 41

From Before to Beyond Time: The Plan of God and Human History 42

Christus Victor: An Integrated Vision for the Christian Life and Witness 44

The Theology of Christus Victor 45

Ladd's View of Time: Living In the Already/Not Yet Kingdom 46

Jesus of Nazareth: The Presence of the Future 47

The Oikos Factor: Spheres of Relationship and Influence 48

Fit To Represent: Multiplying Disciples of the Kingdom of God 49

A Spiritual Warfare Bibliography 50

The Story of God: Our Sacred Roots

The Alpha and the Omega	Christus Victor	Come, Holy Spirit	Your Word is Truth	The Great Confession	His Life in Us	Living in the Way	Reborn to Serve

The LORD God is the source, sustainer, and end of all things in the heavens and earth. All things were formed and exist by his will and for his eternal glory, the triune God, Father, Son, and Holy Spirit, Rom. 11.36

THE TRIUNE GOD'S UNFOLDING DRAMA — God's Self-Revelation in Creation, Israel, and Christ
The Objective Foundation: The Sovereign Love of God
God's narration of his saving work in Christ

THE CHURCH'S PARTICIPATION IN GOD'S UNFOLDING DRAMA — Fidelity to the Apostolic Witness to Christ and his Kingdom
The Subjective Practice: Salvation by Grace through Faith
The Redeemed's joyous response to God's saving work in Christ

The Author of the Story	The Champion of the Story	The Interpreter of the Story	The Testimony of the Story	The People of the Story	Re-enactment of the Story	Embodiment of the Story	Continuation of the Story
The Father As *Director*	Jesus As *Lead Actor*	The Spirit As *Narrator*	Scripture As *Script*	As Saints, *Confessors*	As Worshipers, *Ministers*	As Followers, *Sojourners*	As Servants, *Ambassadors*
Christian *Worldview*	Communal *Identity*	Spiritual *Experience*	Biblical *Authority*	Orthodox *Theology*	Priestly *Worship*	Congregational *Discipleship*	Kingdom *Witness*
Theistic and Trinitarian Vision	Christ-centered Foundation	Spirit-indwelt and -filled Community	Canonical and Apostolic Witness	Ancient Creedal Affirmation of Faith	Weekly Gathering in Christian Assembly	Corporate, Ongoing Spiritual Formation	Active Agents of the Reign of God
Sovereign Willing	Messianic Representing	Divine Comforting	Inspired Testifying	Truthful Retelling	Joyful Excelling	Faithful Indwelling	Hopeful Compelling
Creator True Maker of the cosmos	**Recapitulation** *typos* and Fulfillment of the Covenant	**Life-Giver** Regeneration and Adoption	**Divine Inspiration** God-breathed Word	**The Confession of Faith** Union with Christ	**Song and Celebration** Historical Recitation	**Pastoral Oversight** Shepherding the Flock	**Explicit Unity** Love for the Saints
Owner Sovereign Disposer of creation	**Revealer** Incarnation of the Word	**Teacher** Illuminator of the Truth	**Sacred History** Historical Record	**Baptism into Christ** Communion of Saints	**Homilies and Teachings** Prophetic Proclamation	**Shared Spirituality** Common Journey through the Spiritual Disciplines	**Radical Hospitality** Evidence of God's Kingdom Reign
Ruler Blessed Controller of all things	**Redeemer** Reconciler of all things	**Helper** Endowment and the Power	**Biblical Theology** Divine Commentary	**The Rule of Faith** the Apostles' Creed and the Nicene Creed	**The Lord's Supper** Dramatic Re-enactment	**Embodiment** *anamnesis* and *prolepsis* through the Church Year	**Extravagant Generosity** Good Works
Covenant Keeper Faithful Promisor	**Restorer** Christ, the Victor over the powers of evil	**Guide** Divine Presence and Shekinah	**Spiritual Food** Sustenance for the Journey	**The Vincentian Canon** Ubiquity, antiquity, universality	**Eschatological Foreshadowing** The Already and Not Yet	**Effective Discipling** Spiritual Formation in the Believing Assembly	**Evangelical Witness** Making Disciples of All People Groups

From Before to Beyond Time:

The Plan of God and Human History

Adapted from Suzanne de Dietrich. **God's Unfolding Purpose.** *Philadelphia: Westminster Press, 1976.*

I.   Before Time (Eternity Past) 1 Cor. 2.7
   A.   The Eternal Triune God
   B.   God's Eternal Purpose
   C.   The Mystery of Iniquity
   D.   The Principalities and Powers

II.   Beginning of Time (Creation and Fall) Gen. 1.1
   A.   Creative Word
   B.   Humanity
   C.   Fall
   D.   Reign of Death and First Signs of Grace

III.   Unfolding of Time (God's Plan Revealed Through Israel) Gal. 3.8
   A.   Promise (Patriarchs)
   B.   Exodus and Covenant at Sinai
   C.   Promised Land
   D.   The City, the Temple, and the Throne (Prophet, Priest, and King)
   E.   Exile
   F.   Remnant

IV.   Fullness of Time (Incarnation of the Messiah) Gal. 4.4-5
   A.   The King Comes to His Kingdom
   B.   The Present Reality of His Reign
   C.   The Secret of the Kingdom: the Already and the Not Yet
   D.   The Crucified King
   E.   The Risen Lord

V.   The Last Times (The Descent of the Holy Spirit) Acts 2.16-18
   A.   Between the Times: the Church as Foretaste of the Kingdom
   B.   The Church as Agent of the Kingdom
   C.   The Conflict Between the Kingdoms of Darkness and Light

VI.   The Fulfillment of Time (The Second Coming) Matt. 13.40-43
   A.   The Return of Christ
   B.   Judgment
   C.   The Consummation of His Kingdom

VII.   Beyond Time (Eternity Future) 1 Cor. 15.24-28
   A.   Kingdom Handed Over to God the Father
   B.   God as All in All

From Before to Beyond Time
Scriptures for Major Outline Points

I. Before Time (Eternity Past)

1 Cor. 2.7 (ESV) - But we impart a secret and hidden wisdom of God, *which God decreed before the ages* for our glory (cf. Titus 1.2).

II. Beginning of Time (Creation and Fall)

Gen. 1.1 (ESV) - *In the beginning*, God created the heavens and the earth.

III. Unfolding of Time (God's Plan Revealed Through Israel)

Gal. 3.8 (ESV) - And the Scripture, foreseeing that God would justify the Gentiles by faith, *preached the Gospel beforehand to Abraham*, saying, "In you shall all the nations be blessed" (cf. Rom. 9.4-5).

IV. Fullness of Time (The Incarnation of the Messiah)

Gal. 4.4-5 (ESV) - *But when the fullness of time had come*, God sent forth his Son, born of woman, born under the law, to redeem those who were under the law, so that we might receive adoption as sons.

V. The Last Times (The Descent of the Holy Spirit)

Acts 2.16-18 (ESV) - But this is what was uttered through the prophet Joel: "'*And in the last days it shall be*,' God declares, 'that I will pour out my Spirit on all flesh, and your sons and your daughters shall prophesy, and your young men shall see visions, and your old men shall dream dreams; even on my male servants and female servants in those days I will pour out my Spirit, and they shall prophesy.'"

VI. The Fulfillment of Time (The Second Coming)

Matt. 13.40-43 (ESV) - Just as the weeds are gathered and burned with fire, *so will it be at the close of the age*. The Son of Man will send his angels, and they will gather out of his Kingdom all causes of sin and all lawbreakers, and throw them into the fiery furnace. In that place there will be weeping and gnashing of teeth. Then the righteous will shine like the sun in the Kingdom of their Father. He who has ears, let him hear.

VII. Beyond Time (Eternity Future)

1 Cor. 15.24-28 (ESV) - Then comes the end, when he delivers the Kingdom to God the Father after destroying every rule and every authority and power. For he must reign until he has put all his enemies under his feet. The last enemy to be destroyed is death. For "God has put all things in subjection under his feet." But when it says, "all things are put in subjection," it is plain that he is excepted who put all things in subjection under him. When all things are subjected to him, then the Son himself will also be subjected to him who put all things in subjection under him, that God may be all in all.

Christus Victor: An Integrated Vision for the Christian Life and Witness

Rev. Dr. Don L. Davis

Christus Victor

*Destroyer of Evil and Death
Restorer of Creation
Victor o'er Hades and Sin
Crusher of Satan*

For Theology and Doctrine

- The authoritative Word of Christ's victory: the Apostolic Tradition: the Holy Scriptures
- Theology as commentary on the grand narrative of God
- Christus Victor as core theological framework for meaning in the world
- The Nicene Creed: the Story of God's triumphant grace

For Spirituality

- The Holy Spirit's presence and power in the midst of God's people
- Sharing in the disciplines of the Spirit
- Gatherings, lectionary, liturgy, and our observances in the Church Year
- Living the life of the risen Christ in the rhythm of our ordinary lives

For Worship

- People of the Resurrection: unending celebration of the people of God
- Remembering, participating in the Christ event in our worship
- Listen and respond to the Word
- Transformed at the Table, the Lord's Supper
- The presence of the Father through the Son in the Spirit

For the Church

- The Church is the primary extension of Jesus in the world
- Ransomed treasure of the victorious, risen Christ
- Laos: The people of God
- God's new creation: presence of the future
- Locus and agent of the Already/NotYet Kingdom

For Gifts

- God's gracious endowments and benefits from Christus Victor
- Pastoral offices to the Church
- The Holy Spirit's sovereign dispensing of the gifts
- Stewardship: divine, diverse gifts for the common good

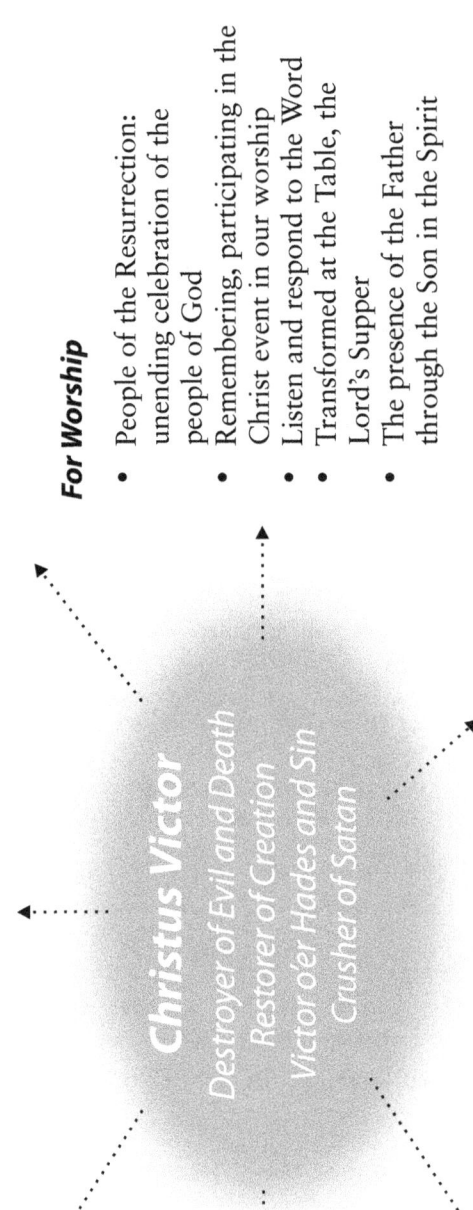

For Evangelism and Mission

- Evangelism as unashamed declaration and demonstration of Christus Victor to the world
- The Gospel as Good News of kingdom pledge
- We proclaim God's Kingdom come in the person of Jesus of Nazareth
- The Great Commission: go to all people groups making disciples of Christ and his Kingdom
- Proclaiming Christ as Lord and Messiah

For Justice and Compassion

- The gracious and generous expressions of Jesus through the Church
- The Church displays the very life of the Kingdom
- The Church demonstrates the very life of the Kingdom of heaven right here and now
- Having freely received, we freely give (no sense of merit or pride)
- Justice as tangible evidence of the Kingdom come

The Theology of Christus Victor

Rev. Dr. Don L. Davis

	The Promised Messiah	The Word Made Flesh	The Son of Man	The Suffering Servant	The Lamb of God	The Victorious Conqueror	The Reigning Lord in Heaven	The Bridegroom and Coming King
Biblical Framework	Israel's hope of Yahweh's anointed who would redeem his people	In the person of Jesus of Nazareth, the Lord has come to the world	As the promised king and divine Son of Man, Jesus reveals the Father's glory and salvation to the world	As Inaugurator of the Kingdom of God, Jesus demonstrates God's reign present through his words, wonders, and works	As both High Priest and Paschal Lamb, Jesus offers himself to God on our behalf as a sacrifice for sin	In his resurrection from the dead and ascension to God's right hand, Jesus is proclaimed as Victor over the power of sin and death	Now reigning at God's right hand till his enemies are made his footstool, Jesus pours out his benefits on his body	Soon the risen and ascended Lord will return to gather his Bride, the Church, and consummate his work
Scripture References	Isa. 9.6-7 Jer. 23.5-6 Isa. 11.1-10	John 1.14-18 Matt. 1.20-23 Phil. 2.6-8	Matt. 2.1-11 Num. 24.17 Luke 1.78-79	Mark 1.14-15 Matt. 12.25-30 Luke 17.20-21	2 Cor. 5.18-21 Isa. 52-53 John 1.29	Eph. 1.16-23 Phil. 2.5-11 Col. 1.15-20	1 Cor. 15.25 Eph. 4.15-16 Acts 2.32-36	Rom. 14.7-9 Rev. 5.9-13 1 Thess. 4.13-18
Jesus' History	The pre-incarnate, only begotten Son of God in glory	His conception by the Spirit, and birth to Mary	His manifestation to the magi and to the world	His teaching, exorcisms, miracles, and mighty works among the people	His suffering, crucifixion, death, and burial	His resurrection, with appearances to his witnesses, and his ascension to the Father	The sending of the Holy Spirit and his gifts, and Christ's session in heaven at the Father's right hand	His soon return from heaven to earth as Lord and Christ the Second Coming
Description	The biblical promise for the seed of Abraham, the prophet like Moses, the son of David	In the incarnation, God has come to us. Jesus reveals to humankind the Father's glory in fullness	In Jesus, God has shown his salvation to the entire world, including the Gentiles	In Jesus, the promised Kingdom of God has come visibly to earth, demonstrating his binding of Satan and rescinding the Curse	As God's perfect Lamb, Jesus offers himself up to God as a sin offering on behalf of the entire world	In his resurrection and ascension, Jesus destroyed death, disarmed Satan, and rescinded the curse	Jesus is installed at the Father's right hand as Head of the Church, Firstborn from the dead, and supreme Lord in heaven	As we labor in his harvest field in the world, so we await Christ's return, the fulfillment of his promise
Church Year	Advent	Christmas	Season after Epiphany: *Baptism and Transfiguration*	Lent	Holy Week: *Passion*	Eastertide: *Easter, Ascension Day, Pentecost*	Season after Pentecost: *Trinity Sunday*	Season after Pentecost: *All Saints Day, Reign of Christ the King*
	The Coming of Christ	*The Birth of Christ*	*The Manifestation of Christ*	*The Ministry of Christ*	*The Suffering and Death of Christ*	*The Resurrection and Ascension of Christ*	*The Heavenly Session of Christ*	*The Reign of Christ*
Spiritual Formation	As we await his Coming, let us proclaim and affirm the hope of Christ	O Word made flesh, let us every heart prepare him room to dwell	Divine Son of Man, show the nations your salvation and glory	In the person of Christ, the power of the reign of God has come to earth and to the Church	May those who share the Lord's death be resurrected with him	Let us participate by faith in the victory of Christ over the power of sin, Satan, and death	Come, indwell us, Holy Spirit, and empower us to advance Christ's Kingdom in the world	We live and work in expectation of his soon return, seeking to please him in all things

Ladd's View of Time

Rev. Dr. Don L. Davis

The Spirit: The pledge of the inheritance (*arrabon*)
The Church: The foretaste (*aparche*) of the Kingdom
"In Christ": The rich life (*en Christos*) we share as citizens of the Kingdom

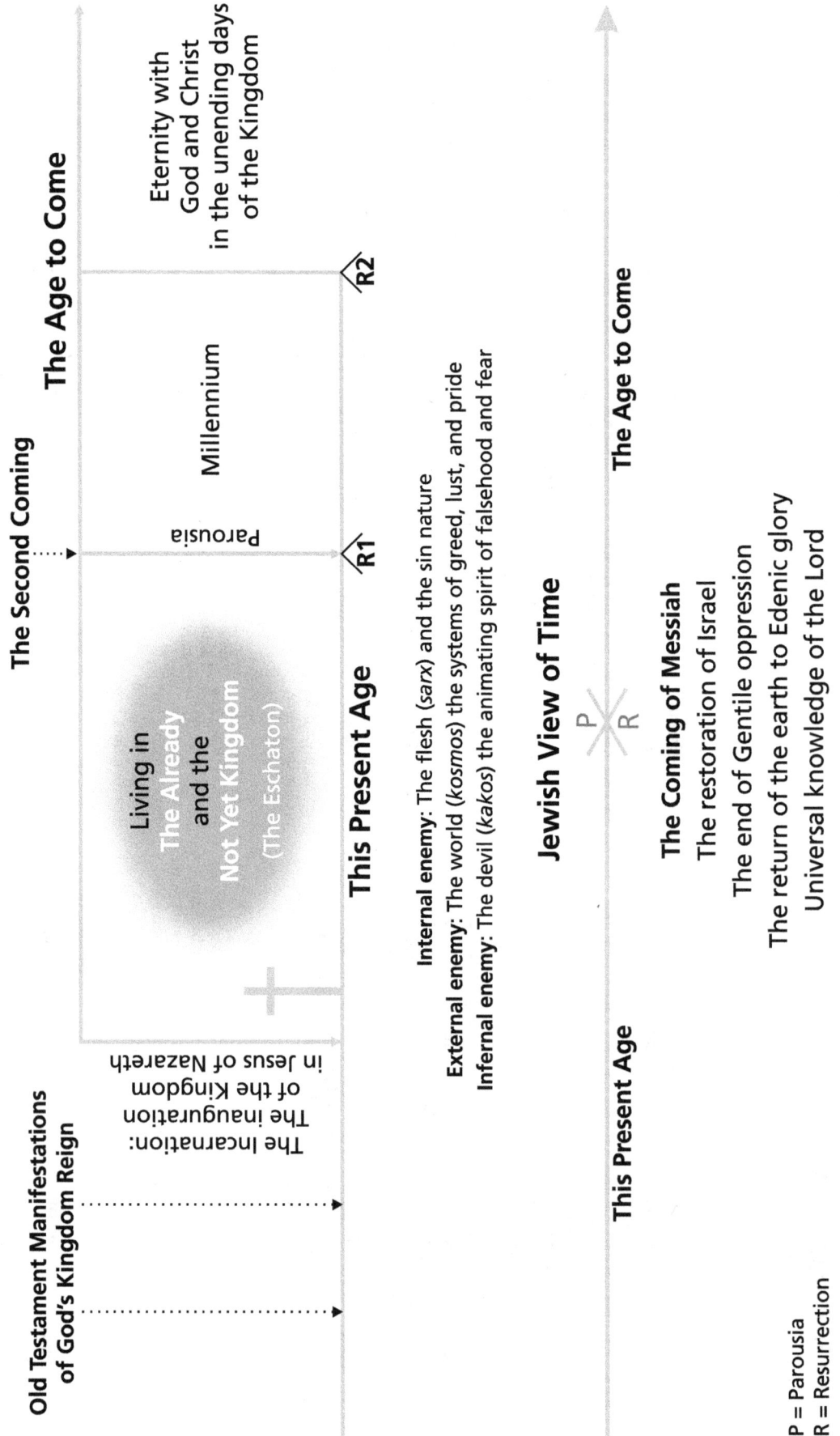

The Second Coming

The Age to Come

Eternity with
God and Christ
in the unending days
of the Kingdom

Millennium

Parousia

R2

R1

Living in
The Already
and the
Not Yet Kingdom
(The Eschaton)

The Incarnation:
The inauguration
of the Kingdom
in Jesus of Nazareth

This Present Age

**Old Testament Manifestations
of God's Kingdom Reign**

Internal enemy: The flesh (*sarx*) and the sin nature
External enemy: The world (*kosmos*) the systems of greed, lust, and pride
Infernal enemy: The devil (*kakos*) the animating spirit of falsehood and fear

Jewish View of Time

P
R

The Coming of Messiah
The restoration of Israel
The end of Gentile oppression
The return of the earth to Edenic glory
Universal knowledge of the Lord

The Age to Come

This Present Age

P = Parousia
R = Resurrection

Jesus of Nazareth: The Presence of the Future

Rev. Dr. Don L. Davis

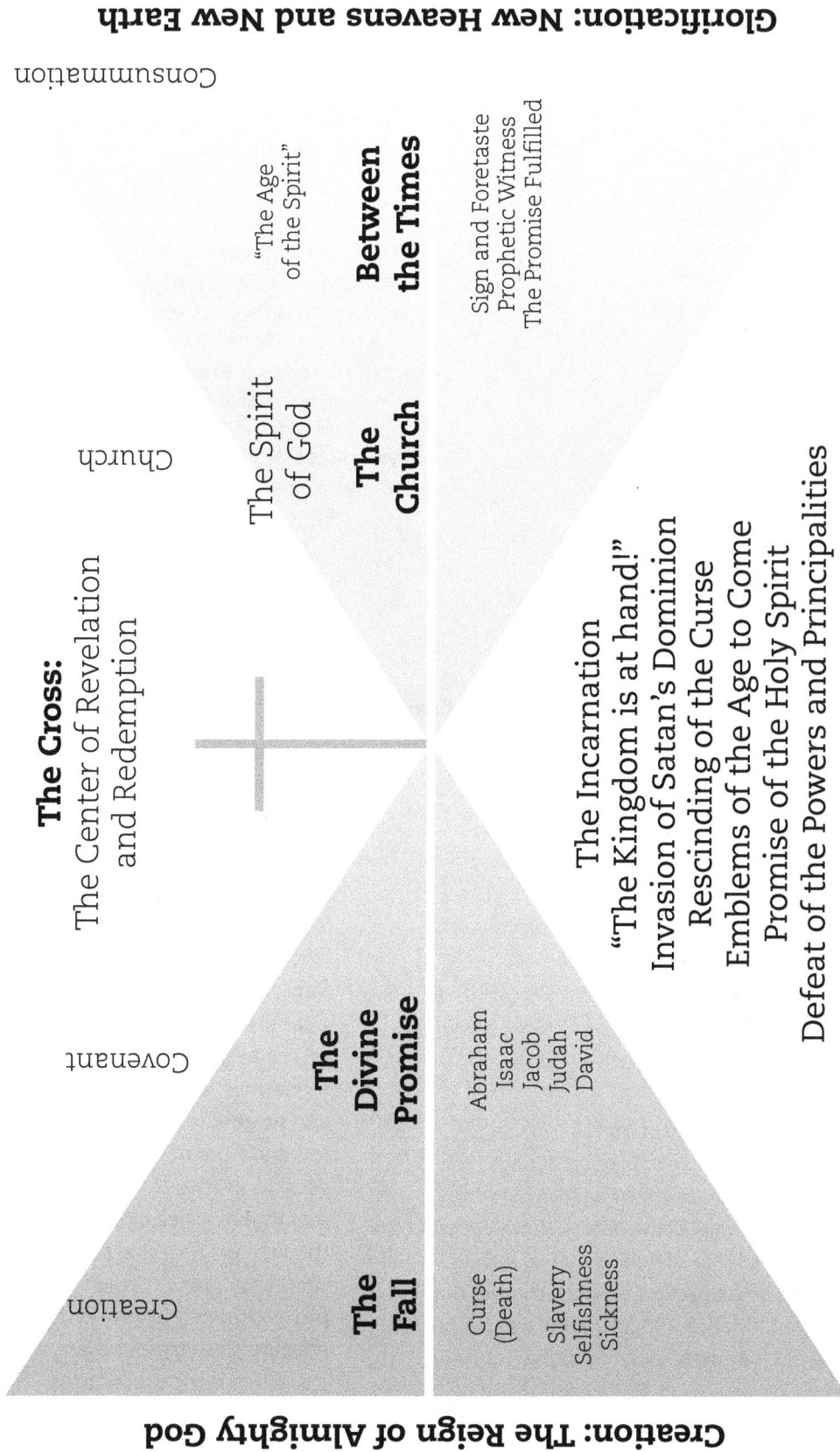

Glorification: New Heavens and New Earth

Consummation

Church

Covenant

Creation

Creation: The Reign of Almighty God

The Cross:
The Center of Revelation and Redemption

The Spirit of God

The Church

Between the Times

"The Age of the Spirit"

Sign and Foretaste
Prophetic Witness
The Promise Fulfilled

The Incarnation
"The Kingdom is at hand!"
Invasion of Satan's Dominion
Rescinding of the Curse
Emblems of the Age to Come
Promise of the Holy Spirit
Defeat of the Powers and Principalities

The Divine Promise

Abraham
Isaac
Jacob
Judah
David

The Fall

Curse (Death)

Slavery
Selfishness
Sickness

The *Oikos* Factor: Spheres of Relationship and Influence

Rev. Dr. Don L. Davis

Survey: 42,000 asked: Who or what was responsible for your coming to Christ and your church:

Special need	1-2%
Walk-in	2-3%
Pastor	5-6%
Visitation	1-2%
Sunday School	4-5%
Evangelistic crusade/TV	1/2%
Church program	2-3%
Friend or relative	75-90%!!

--Church Growth, Inc. Monrovia, CA

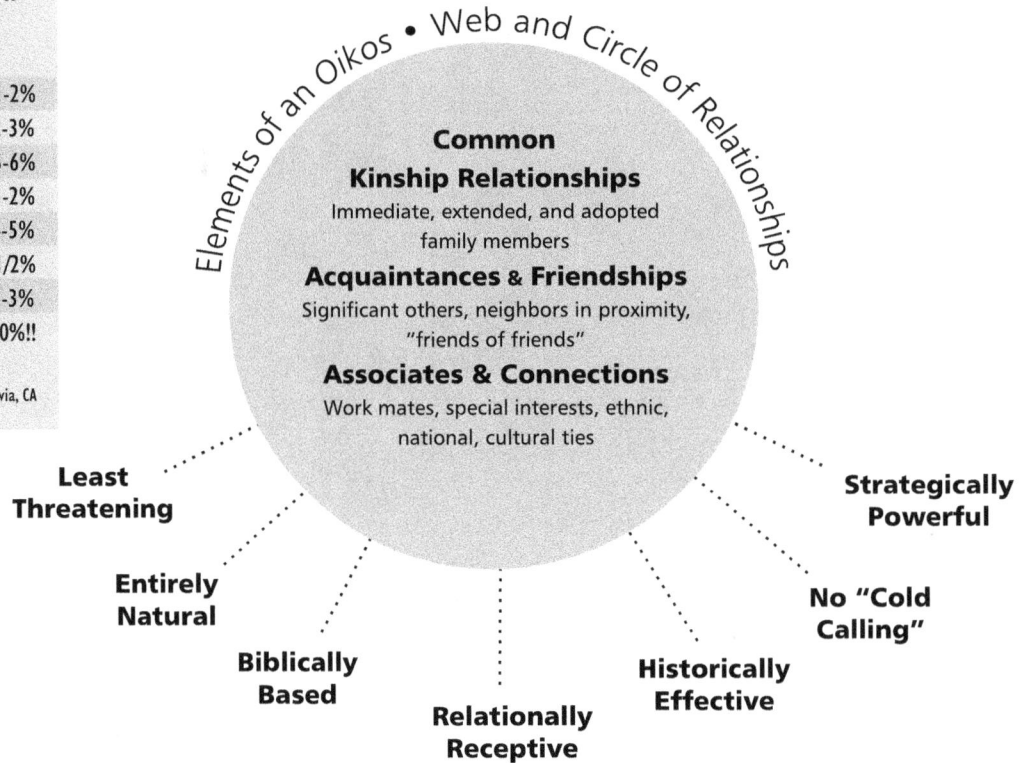

Elements of an Oikos • Web and Circle of Relationships

Common Kinship Relationships
Immediate, extended, and adopted family members

Acquaintances & Friendships
Significant others, neighbors in proximity, "friends of friends"

Associates & Connections
Work mates, special interests, ethnic, national, cultural ties

Least Threatening

Strategically Powerful

Entirely Natural

No "Cold Calling"

Biblically Based

Historically Effective

Relationally Receptive

Oikos (household) in the OT

"A household usually contained four generations, including men, married women, unmarried daughters, slaves of both sexes, persons without citizenship, and "sojourners," or resident foreign workers." – Hans Walter Wolff, Anthology of the Old Testament.

Oikos (household) in the NT

Evangelism and disciple making in our NT narratives are often described as following the flow of the relational networks of various people within their *oikoi* (households), that is, those natural lines of connection in which they resided and lived (c.f., Mark 5.19; Luke 19.9; John 4.53; 1.41-45, etc.). Andrew to Simon (John 1.41-45), and both Cornelius (Acts 10-11) and the Philippian jailer (Acts 16) are notable cases of evangelism and discipling through *oikoi*.

Oikos (household) among the urban poor

While great differences exist between cultures, kinship relationships, special interest groups, and family structures among urban populations, it is clear that urbanites connect with others far more on the basis of connections through relationships, friendships, and family than through proximity and neighborhood alone. Often times the closest friends of urban poor dwellers are not immediately close by in terms of neighborhood; family and friends may dwell blocks, even miles away. Taking the time to study the precise linkages of relationships among the dwellers in a certain area can prove extremely helpful in determining the most effective strategies for evangelism and disciple making in inner city contexts.

Fit to Represent: Multiplying Disciples of the Kingdom of God

Rev. Dr. Don L. Davis

Luke 10.16 (ESV) - The one who hears you hears me, and the one who rejects you rejects me, and the one who rejects me rejects him who sent me.

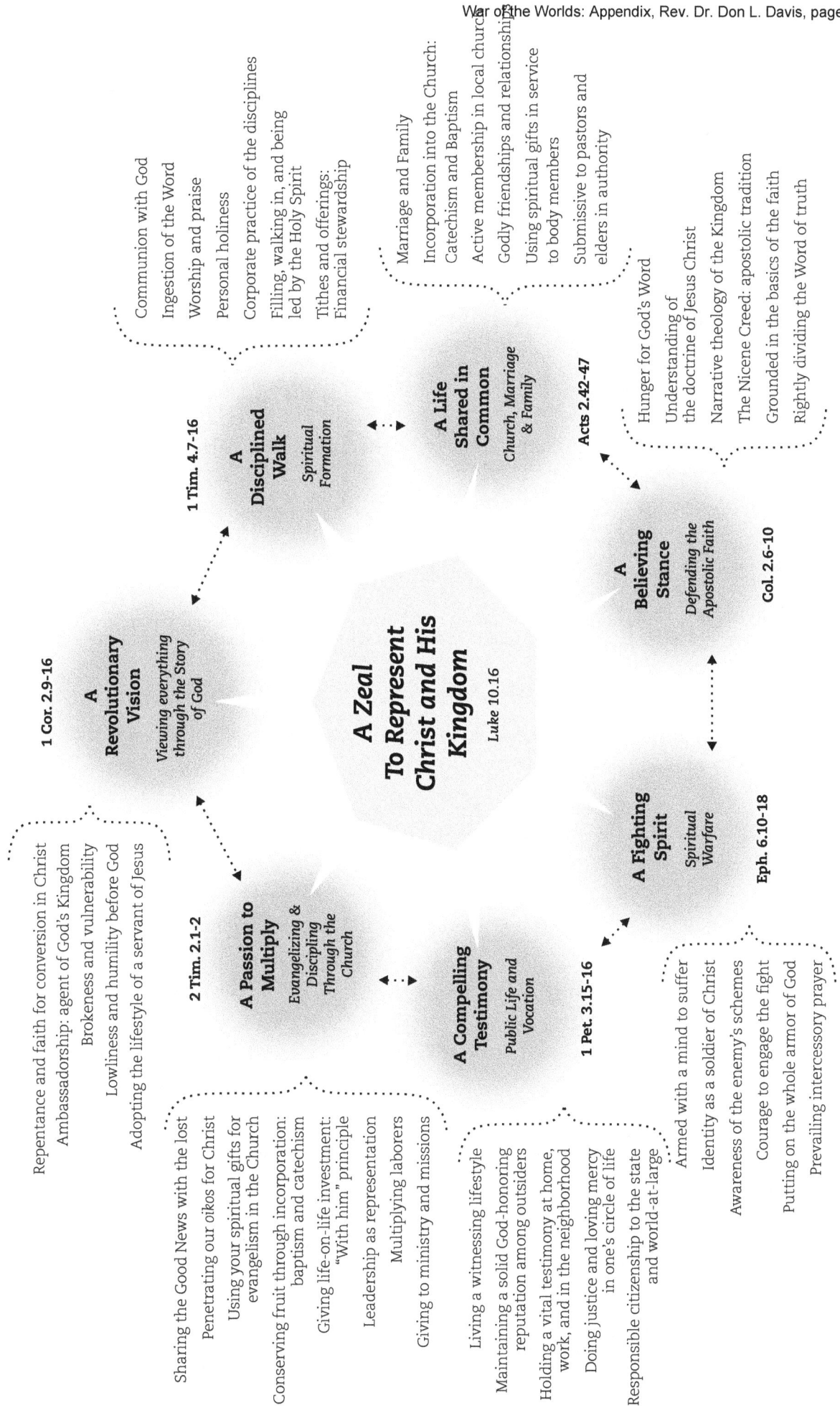

A Zeal To Represent Christ and His Kingdom
Luke 10.16

A Revolutionary Vision
Viewing everything through the Story of God
1 Cor. 2.9-16

A Disciplined Walk
Spiritual Formation
1 Tim. 4.7-16

- Communion with God
- Ingestion of the Word
- Worship and praise
- Personal holiness
- Corporate practice of the disciplines
- Filling, walking in, and being led by the Holy Spirit
- Tithes and offerings: Financial stewardship

A Life Shared in Common
Church, Marriage & Family
Acts 2.42-47

- Marriage and Family
- Incorporation into the Church: Catechism and Baptism
- Active membership in local church
- Godly friendships and relationships
- Using spiritual gifts in service to body members
- Submissive to pastors and elders in authority

A Believing Stance
Defending the Apostolic Faith
Col. 2.6-10

- Hunger for God's Word
- Understanding of the doctrine of Jesus Christ
- Narrative theology of the Kingdom
- The Nicene Creed: apostolic tradition
- Grounded in the basics of the faith
- Rightly dividing the Word of truth

A Fighting Spirit
Spiritual Warfare
Eph. 6.10-18

- Armed with a mind to suffer
- Identity as a soldier of Christ
- Awareness of the enemy's schemes
- Courage to engage the fight
- Putting on the whole armor of God
- Prevailing intercessory prayer

A Compelling Testimony
Public Life and Vocation
1 Pet. 3.15-16

- Living a witnessing lifestyle
- Maintaining a solid God-honoring reputation among outsiders
- Holding a vital testimony at home, work, and in the neighborhood
- Doing justice and loving mercy in one's circle of life
- Responsible citizenship to the state and world-at-large

A Passion to Multiply
Evangelizing & Discipling Through the Church
2 Tim. 2.1-2

- Sharing the Good News with the lost
- Penetrating our oikos for Christ
- Using your spiritual gifts for evangelism in the Church
- Conserving fruit through incorporation: baptism and catechism
- Giving life-on-life investment: "With him" principle
- Leadership as representation
- Multiplying laborers
- Giving to ministry and missions

(Revolutionary Vision list)
- Repentance and faith for conversion in Christ
- Ambassadorship: agent of God's Kingdom
- Brokenness and vulnerability
- Lowliness and humility before God
- Adopting the lifestyle of a servant of Jesus

© 2007. The Urban Ministry Institute. www.tumi.org. TUMI is a ministry of World Impact, Inc.

A Spiritual Warfare Bibliography

Anderson, Dr. Neil T. *Released from Bondage.* San Bernardino, CA: Here's Life Publishers, 1991.
-----. *The Bondage Breaker.* Eugene, OR: Harvest House Publishers, 1993.

Arn, Win and Charles Arn. *The Master's Plan for Making Disciples.* 2nd Ed. Grand Rapids: Baker Book House, 1998.

Billheimer, Paul. *Destined for the Throne.* Minneapolis: Bethany House, 1975.

-----. *Destined to Overcome.* Minneapolis: Bethany House Publishers, 1982.

Eims, Leroy. *The Lost Art of Disciple Making.* Grand Rapids, MI: Zondervan Publishing House, 1978.

Epp, Theodore H. *The Believer's Spiritual Warfare.* Lincoln: Back to the Bible, 1973.

Dawson, John. *Taking Our Cities for God.* Lake Mary, FL: Creation House, 1989.

Grounds, Vernon. *Radical Commitment: Getting Serious About Christian Growth.* Portland, OR: Multnomah Press, 1984.

Hayford, Jack. *Answering the Call to Evangelism (Spirit Filled Life Kingdom Dynamics Study Guides).* Nashville: Thomas Nelson Publishers, 1995.

Holly, James L. M.D. *The Basis of Victory in Spiritual Warfare: The Blood of Jesus Christ.* Beaumont, TX: Mission and Ministry to Men, Inc, 1992.

Ladd, George Eldon. *The Gospel of the Kingdom.* Grand Rapids: Eerdmans, 1999.

MacArther, John Jr. *The Believer's Armor.* Chicago, IL: Moody Press, 1986.

McAlpine, Thomas H. *Facing the Powers: What are the Options?* Eugene, OR: Wipf and Stock Publishers, 2003.

Murphy, Ed. *The Handbook for Spiritual Warfare.* Revised and updated. Nashville: Thomas Nelson Publishers, 2003.

Ortiz, Juan Carlos. *Disciple.* Carol Stream, IL: Creation House, 1982.

Phillips, Keith. *Out of Ashes.* Los Angeles: World Impact Press, 1996.

Pirolo, Neal and Yvonne. *Prepare for Battle: Basic Training in Spiritual Warfare.* San Diego, CA: Emmaus Road, International, 1997.

Shenk, David W. and Ervin R. Stutzman. *Creating Communities of the Kingdom.* Scottsdale, PA: Herald Press, 1998.

Snyder, Howard A. *Kingdom, Church, and World.* Eugene, OR: Wipf and Stock Publishers, 1985.

Stedman, Ray C. *Spiritual Warfare.* Waco, TX: Word Books, 1975.

Stratford, Lauren. *Satan's Underground.* Eugene, OR: Harvest House Publishers, 1988

Tippit, Sammy. *Fit for Battle: The Character, Weapons, and Strategies of the Spiritual Warrior.* Chicago, IL: Moody Press, 1994.

Trask, Thomas E. And Goodall, Wayde I. *The Battle: Defeating the Enemies of Your Soul.* Grand Rapids, MI: Zondervan Publishing House, 1997.

Warner, Timothy M. *Spiritual Warfare: Victory of the Powers of This Dark World.* Wheaton: Crossway Books, 1991.

White, Thomas B. *The Believer's Guide to Spiritual Warfare.* Ann Arbor, MI: Servant Publications, 1990.

9 781629 327099